iPhone 12 Tips and Tricks

An illustrated Guide on How to Master iOS 14 and iPhone 12 Series (iPhone 12, Pro and Max)

Jessica Peters

TABLE OF CONTENTS

Introduction

Apple unveiled its latest flagship iPhones, iPhone 12, 12 mini, Pro, and Pro Max on October 13, 2020, which offers amazing features at an affordable price tag. The iPhone 12 and 12 mini, are perfect for anyone who doesn't need the Pro camera features.

The 6.1-inch iPhone 12 is a sequel to iPhone 11, while the 5.4-inch is an all-new size and is the smallest iPhone Apple has released since the iPhone SE in 2016. The two phones are technically similar, aside from the screen and battery size. For the first time in years, iPhone features Super Retina XDR OLED displays with a design on both edges but with the exception of the Face ID notch and tiny bezels around the edge. The displays offer HDR support with 1200 nits of peak brightness, Large Color for vibrant, true-to-life colors, Haptic Touch for feedback, and True Tone to fit the color temperature of the display to the ambient lighting for a more realistic viewing experience.

This year, Apple revamped the design of the iPhone 12 lineup, introducing smooth edges that are a departure from previous models' rounded edges and are identical in design to the iPad Pro. There is a new A14 processor within the iPhone and it is the first of its kind designed on a 5-nanometer process for improvements in performance and quality.

CHAPTER ONE: GETTING STARTED

Battery Life and Charging

iPhone 12 offers fast charging, which uses a 20W power adapter to provide a 50% charge in 30mins. Apple launched MagSafe accessories on this new device, designed to operate with a ring of magnets. MagSafe has a charger, an iPhone case, and a pocket accessory. All iPhone 12 models provide up to "17hrs" of video playback, "11hrs" of video streaming, and "65hrs" of audio playback. The iPhone 12 mini has a shorter battery life since it is has a smaller battery.

Turn On and Set-Up

In one of three ways, you can set up your iPhone 12, start new, restore it from another iPhone, or import content from a non-Apple phone. Here's what each of those choices means.

- Set up as new: It means getting all started from scratch. This is for people who want to feel completely brand new with their device.

- Restore from a previous iPhone: This can be done with iCloud online, USB (with iTunes), or Finder (macOS Catalina). This is for those who want all their files on the new iOS device when switching from their previous one.

- Import from Android or Windows Phone: Apple has an online app in Google Play that allows you to move files from any old device.

The first time you turn your device on, you will be greeted with "Hello" in several languages. If you start from scratch, restore from an iPhone, or changed from Android, it's all the same.

- Tap slide to configure and slide across the screen to get started.

- Choose your preferred language and select your region.

- Select a Wi-Fi network or instead, use "Cellular". Now", you can decide to use "Automatic Setup" to set up your phone with the same settings as the other iPhones.

To run a manual set up, use the steps below.

- After going through the "Data & Privacy" details for Apple, click "Continue". Again, tap Agree for confirmation.

- Set up Apple Pay, iCloud Keychain, and Siri.

- Tap Send Diagnostic Details to Apple when apps crash or other issues occur, or tap "Don't Send".

- For more visual accessibility, turn on "Display Zoom".

- Tap "Enable Location Services" or you can skip it and enable it later. Tap "Get Started".

If you're setting your device with Face ID, all you have to do is position your face in the camera frame. Then move your head in a circle to reveal all angels.

How to Set Up Cellular Service

- Install a physical Nano-Sim into your iPhone

- Go to Settings, then go to Cellular, then tap Add Cellular Plan.

- Do one of the following:

1. Set up a new plan with your carrier's QR code: Position the iPhone so that the QR code appears in the frame, or manually enter the details. You may be required to enter a confirmation code from your carrier.

2. Install an assigned cellular plan: If you have been notified that a plan has been assigned to you, tap "Carrier Cellular Plan Ready to Be Installed".

3. Transfer a SIM from a previous iPhone to a new one: Select your number from the list. If your number is not available,

make sure you have signed in with the same Apple ID on both iPhones. Not all cellular plans or carriers support the transfer of a SIM to an eSIM.

- Tap Add Cellular Plan. If the new plan is your second line, use the onscreen instructions to configure your plan the way you want.

To switch eSIMs, launch Settings, then go to Cellular, select your preferred plan, then tap "Turn On This Line". You can use a Nano-SIM as your other line if one is available.

How do I manage my cellular plan with Dual Sim?

- Head to Settings, then to Cellular. Next, tap on "Cellular Data" then select a default line. Turn "Allow Cellular Data Switching" on to allow your device to use either line depending on availability and coverage. Roaming charges maybe be incurred if you activated Data Roaming outside the region covered by your carrier's network.

- Tap on "Default Voice Line" and then select a line.

- Tap a line below Cellular Plans, then change some settings such as Calls on Other Devices, Cellular Plan Label, Wi-Fi Calling (if supported), or Sim Pin. The label will be displayed in Messages, Contacts, and Phone.

When using Dual SIM, note the following:

- For your device to receive another call when one of the lines is already on a call, you must enable Wi-Fi Calling. If there is no Wi-Fi connection when you receive a second call on the other line, your phone will make use of the cellular data of the line currently on call to receive the other call. This might attract charges. To receive the new incoming call, you must permit data usage on the line currently on-call (turn "Allow Cellular Data Switching" on)

- If "Wi-Fi Calling" for a line is not on, all incoming phone calls on that line (plus emergency services calls) will go to your voicemail (if supported by your carrier).

- If call forwarding is not supported and you set it up, your calls won't go to voicemail when one line is busy or out of service. Cellular availability depends on your location, wireless network, and iPhone model.

How to Connect to the Internet

- Via a Wi-Fi network: You can use your computer and some equipment from your Internet provider to configure a Wi-Fi connection at home. Or, you can connect your iPhone to a hotspot. You can discover and connect to a hotspot from cafés, libraries, hotels, and transportation centers.

- You can connect via a data network (4G or 5G) as long as you have cellphone coverage. To enable data access, go to Settings, to General, and then go to Network. Turn 4G or 5G on and Cellular Data settings.

How to connect to a Wi-Fi network.

- Head to settings, turn your Wi-Fi on, and choose from the available networks to connect to.

- After you select a network, enter your password (if there is any).

- Type the password and tap Join. You are connected.

How to Manage Apple ID and Cloud Settings

Your Apple ID account is what you'll use to access Apple services such as iTunes and App Store, Apple Books, etc. You can store and share your apps, photos, documents, videos, music, and more on iCloud and keep your files updated on all your devices.

How to set up iCloud

You'll be asked if you want to use iCloud Drive to store your data when you update your iOS operating system or start using a new iPhone. If you tap 'Yes,' then you are all set. If during setup, you have tapped "No" but you have decided to use iCloud Drive, you can still manually activate it.

- Go to setting and tap on your Apple ID banner.
- Tap iCloud. Switch on the iCloud Drive and log in with your iCloud account.

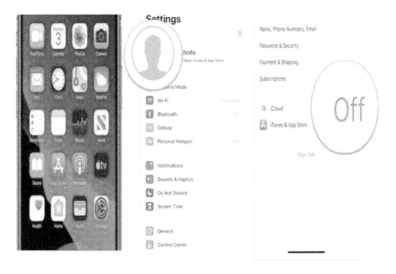

How to view your iCloud account info

You can view your contact details, registered devices, security, and iCloud payment setup.

- Go to setting and tap on your Apple ID banner. Scroll down and select a device you want to view or remove from your account. Tap on "Remove from Account".

- Scroll up and tap the details you want to change. You can change your name, phone number, email address, birthday, password, registered phone number.

- Tap on "Payment & Shipping" to change your credit card number, expiration date, and shipping address.

20

How to manage iCloud sync permissions

You can connect to iCloud from third-party apps and access files from any device. You can manually revoke permission at any time even if you used a third-party app to set up iCloud.

- Go to settings and tap on your Apple ID banner.
- Tap iCloud. Here, you can turn the app you want to allow or revoke iCloud Drive syncing on or off.

How to sign out of iCloud

- Go to settings and tap on your Apple ID banner.
- Scroll to Sign Out and tap it. Tap on Sign Out again if prompted.
- To store iCloud data on your device, tap Save on my iPhone or tap "Delete from my iPhone" to delete data.

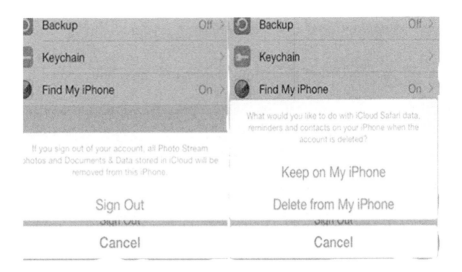

How to Wake and Unlock your iPhone

You can use "raise to wake" to automatically wake your iPhone when you raise to look at it. With this, you can quickly check your notifications, access Control Center, swipe left to take a picture, or swipe right to for widgets.

- Head to Settings and tap on Display & Brightness. Tap on the Raise to Wake switch it on or off.

CHAPTER TWO: BASIC GUIDE

Cameras

iPhone 12 has sets of 12mp cameras. iPhone 12 and 12 mini each have a 12mp front camera, 12mp wide-angle, and standard cameras. A 12mp 2x zoom and a LiDAR scanner are added to the 12 Pro, while the Pro Max has 2.5x zoom and LiDAR. LiDAR bounces light pulses off objects to determine distance. It makes augmented-reality apps more fluid; when taking pictures, it speeds up and improves autofocus in dim light and enables the 12 Pro's striking low-light portrait mode.

Alas, Apple's Night mode takes out most of its competition. The 12 Pro's 2x zoom gives clarity that is impossible with iPhone 12 and 11 digital zoom and is even a little better than the Galaxy Note 20. The real difference is in Night Mode. iPhone 12 series supports the night mode on its front cameras. iPhone 12 in short, provides very good cameras. If you are unhappy with the low light performance of your older device, you will experience a better upgrade with this new device. iPhone 12 also supports Dolby Vision HDR video recording.

How to Adjust Wallpaper

Wallpapers are a perfect way to add some personality and customization to your phone. And while your images can still be used as wallpapers. It's easy to change your wallpaper, you just need to select the right picture!

- Go to Settings, then to Wallpaper, and then tap on Choose a New Wallpaper. You can choose from Apple's stock images or from your image library.

- Tap the style of wallpaper you wish to use:

1) Dynamic: Choose this is for Apple's stock images with effects that fade into view and react to your phone's movement.

2) Still: For still images.

3) Live: For a Live Photo that will animate after a firm press

4) Photo Library: An image or live photo from your photo library.

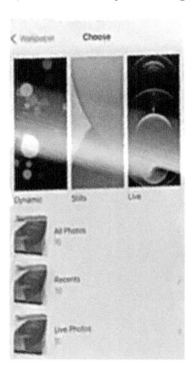

Select your new wallpaper to enter the Preview mode. In Preview mode, you can choose how to show your image. Tap any of the following options:

1. Still: The chosen still image will be displayed as your wallpaper.

2. Perspective: As you move the screen, the still image will change the perspective slightly. (Don't use this if you're prone to motion sickness.)

- Live Photo: If you chose a Live Photo image, this option allows you to animate the image after a firm press.

- Tap Set.

- Tap any of the following option: Set Lock Screen, Set Home Screen or Both

How to change the wallpaper directly from the Photos app

- Go to "Photos" and select an image.

- Tap on the Share button. Find Use as Wallpaper and select it to enter the Preview mode.

- Position the image and zoom it in accordingly.

- Select any of the following options:

1. Still: The chosen still image will be displayed.

2. Perspective: As you move the screen, the still image will change the perspective slightly. (Don't use this if you're prone to motion sickness.)

3. Live Photo: If you chose a Live Photo image, the image will animate after a firm press.

- Tap Set.

- Tap any of the following option: Set Lock Screen, Set Home Screen or Both

How to Turn Dark Mode on And Off

How to activate dark mode with Control Center

This is the fastest way to turn on dark mode.

- Open Control Center on your phone. Swipe down from the top corner or swipe up from the bottom of your screen.

- Firmly press on the screen brightness slider.

- Tap on the "Appearance button" to switch between light and dark.

How to set Dark Mode in Control Center

- Go to Settings, then to "Control Center" and then tap on Customize Controls.

- Tap the '+' sign next to Dark Mode.

- To adjust the location of buttons in the Control Center, tap and drag the handles. Dark Mode will now be available.

How to activate dark mode with Settings

- Head to Settings, then to Display & Brightness, and then tap on Light or Dark to choose an appearance.

- Switch "Automatic" on to automatically switch between light and dark modes.

- Tap "Options" and tap "Sunset to Sunrise" to enable this feature from each sunset until the next sunrise.

- Select "Custom Schedule" to customize the dark mode's time range.

- Tap Light Appearance to select when to activate the light mode.

- Tap Dark Appearance to select when to activate the dark mode. That's it.

How to Adjust Screen Brightness and Color

Your screen brightness level can affect your iPhone's battery life. By default, iOS will automatically adjust the phone's brightness depending on the amount of light the ambient sensor detects. You can also disable auto-brightness to gain full control.

- Launch Settings, then go to Accessibility

- Go to "Display & Text Size" and turn the Auto-Brightness switch off at the bottom. Now, you can do this anytime you need to adjust your screen by opening the Control Center.

How to Magnify Screen with Display Zoom

The 'Enable display zoom' feature works perfectly on the latest iPhones. This awesome feature can be used to automatically enlarge any data on your screen. This feature is pretty useful to enlarge apps like messages, installed apps, contents on your home screen, and more.

Steps

Go to Settings, then to Display and Brightness, and scroll down

- Tap on "View" under the Display Zoom label. Tap on Zoomed and then tap "Set".

- You will get a popup to use Zoomed at the end. So tap on it to apply the feature. Applying this feature will restart your phone.

Now tap the Back button and enjoy this feature on the Mail app, Message app, and as well as Apps icons on the home screen. Zoomed mode makes your contact clearer than the standard screen. Many functions on the iPhone won't work with this feature such as contact pictures in a message. If you are having such kind of issue, then use the Standard display settings. For that, you have to disable Display zoom first.

How to Turn Off Display Zoom on iPhone

Disable the Zoomed screen if you feel your apps are crashing or if they are having stuck and Freeze issues when launched.

- Head to Settings, then tap 'Display & Brightness'. Tap on View under the Display Zoom label.

- Select Standard and tap "Set". Next, you will get a popup to use Standard at the end. So tap on it to apply the feature to regular screen size.

How to Take Screen Shot or Screen Recording

Screenshots are perfect for sharing moments from your favorite videos, high scores, social media conversations, and almost everything you see on your screen. Here's how to take screenshots:

- Open the screen you want to capture. Simultaneously hold the Side button and the Up Volume button to capture.

Before taking screen records, you need to add the option to your Control Center in order to locate the controls easily. Use the steps below.

- Head to Settings, then to Control Center, and scroll to "Screen Recording".

- Tap the + (green plus) logo to add the screen recording controls to your "Control Center".

How to make screen record

- Swipe down from the upper-right corner of the screen and tap the "Screen Record" icon.

- Wait 3 seconds before the recording starts. Your screen recording will start until you stop the recording.

- To stop the screen recording, tap on the red status bar at the top, then tap stop.

- The video will automatically be stored in photos.

By default, there is no audio recorded while you make a screen record. You can add audio along while you record the screen. Here is what to do to add audio:

- Swipe down from the upper-right corner of your screen.

- Hold the Screen Record icon, tap the microphone, and then tap start recording.

- The recording will work now with sound.

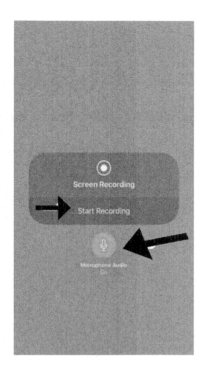

- To stop recording, tap the red status bar on the top left of your screen.

- Tap "Stop". The video will be stored in photos.

Not everything can be recorded. You can't record streaming apps like Netflix otherwise it would be possible to pirate their shows you are streaming. Although, you can record anything including game clips. You can't adjust screen recording settings, you cannot adjust the resolution or video quality of the clip.

How to Multitask With Picture in Picture

This allows users to watch a video on one side while also using other apps or processes. This feature has recently been made available on iOS 14. It works with some apple apps like Safari and Apple TV.

How to use picture in picture

- Load up a video on a supportive app like Safari and go to the full screen.

- You will see an icon on the top left of the phone. Hit the icon and the video will go into picture in picture mode.

- Alternatively, while you are in a full-screen video, you can swipe from the bottom of the iPhone as if you were closing the app. It will enter picture in picture mode.

- Once the video is in picture in picture mode, you can treat the video as if it were a small window. Simply move the video around to get it at the right place on your screen or resize it using pinch gestures.

- If you would like to continue playing the audio, simply swipe the video to the left or right of the screen and the video will be out with the audio still playing. This is extremely useful if you are listening to broadcasts.

It is worth knowing that most videos that are accessible through a browser can be used in picture in picture mode by accessing the videos through Safari.

How to Adjust Volume

You can adjust the ringer volume on your iPhone via Settings or the volume button on the side of your device.

Via Settings

- Head to settings, then go to "Sounds and Haptics."
- Drag the slider under "Ringer and Alerts" to adjust the volume level.

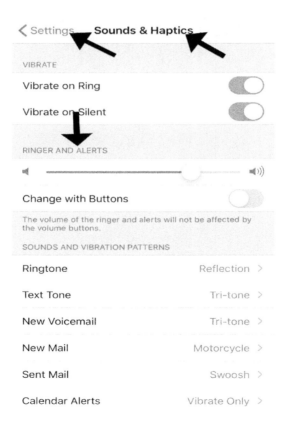

Via Volume buttons

- First go to settings, then go to "Sounds & Haptics."

- Scroll to ringer and alerts, turn on "Change with Buttons"

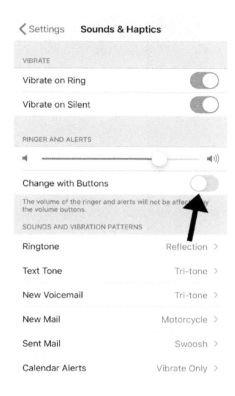

If you enable this feature, the volume buttons will now have two functions:

- Ringer and alerts functions when you are not using media.

- Controls media volume when watching a video or listening to music.

CHAPTER THREE: COMMON SETTINGS

5G Connectivity

iPhone 12 family supports 5G networks, but 5G is sometimes not as fast as the older 4G LTE network. Although the iPhone 12 can switch between networks to save battery life, sometimes the fastest network is not always used.

How to switch between 5G and 4G LTE

I am going to show you how to quickly switch between 5G and 4G LTE. I'll also show you how to speed test both networks so you can see which network is faster. Make sure your Wi-Fi is off.

- Head to settings, to cellular, and then to cellular data options.
- Select "Voice and Data." Change the network to LTE.

Now you have switched the phone to 4G LTE. You can also select the "5G On" network to make the phone run on 5G.

How to see your network speed

Next, we'll look at which network provides the fastest speed.

- Download the SpeedTest app from the Store and launch the app.

- Now tap on "Go."

The app will run a speed test on your downloads and uploads. The test will give you a result at the end which wildly depends on your area. Take note of your results. The results might look something like 80Mbps down and 40Mbps up.

Now go back and test 5G

Now, compare the speed of 4G LTE to 5G. First, switch the phone to 5G. Use the steps provided above to switch to 5G. Now, run the SpeedTest and compare the numbers with your previous result. If the 5G is faster, then leave it. But, if it is slower, you can continue using 4G LTE.

IPhone 12 and IOS 14

IOS 14 is one of the biggest iOS updates to date by Apple, introducing changes to the home screen design, major new features, existing app updates, upgrades to Siri, and several other tweaks that streamline the iOS interface. iOS 14 is now available for use on all compatible devices, so you should see it in Settings at the Software Update section

First off, iOS 14 offers a redesigned Home Screen that supports widgets for the first time. With a Picture in Picture mode, users can simultaneously watch videos or talk on FaceTime while also using other apps. Now, Siri is smarter and can answer a lot of questions with info pulled from the internet. Siri also sends audio messages. Keyboard dictation also runs on the device, offering more privacy layer to the dictated messages.

iOS 14's new Home Screen allows for more customization with the incorporation of widgets, options to hide apps pages, and the new App Library that shows all your apps at a glance. Additional iOS 14 features includes: Translate, home app, air pods, digital car keys, find my, safari, health, the weather app, and accessibility.

How to Move Data from Android to Your iPhone

Switching from Android to iPhone 12 is one of the best upgrades you can make. Luckily, there are several ways to move files from android to iPhone. Am going to give you 2 options to choose from.

Option 1: One-click to transfer data

Your first option is to use a one-stop solution named Phone Transfer. One of its great advantages is that it can transfer almost all important files from android to iPhone 12. This option works on most android phones. Your existing data won't be erased from the device during transfer making it very useful. Follow these steps to use phone transfer:

- Connect the android to your computer via USB and turn USB debugging mode on.

- Connect the new iPhone to the machine and tap Trust whenever it pops up.

- Mark the files you want to move and click Start Copy. Wait until the transfer is completed.

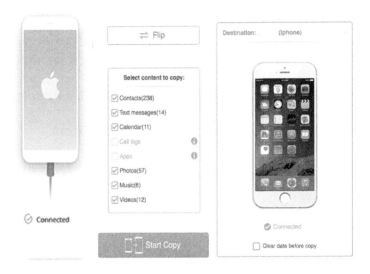

Note: Using phone transfer does not let you transfer App data.

Option 2: Move to iOS

Apple has its own app called "Move to iOS" to help its users transfer files from android to iPhone via Wi-Fi. You can securely move movies, contacts, pictures, videos, messages, mail accounts, web bookmarks, and calendar.

First, you have to install the app on both devices then follow these steps:

- Set up your new iPhone until you get to the Apps & Data screen.

- Tap on "Move Data from Android". On your android, download the 'Move to iOS app' and launch it.

- Tap agree after going through the T&C, then tap "Next" in the find your code screen.

- Tap Continue on your iPhone as well and wait until a code appears.

- Enter the code that appears on your Android. Your Android will connect with your iPhone via Wi-Fi.

- Mark the files you want to move and then tap Next.

Enter Code

To continue setup, enter the code from your iPhone or iPad:

I have a 10 digit code

1	2	3
4	5	6
7	8	9
	0	⌫

Next >

Transfer Data

Choose what you would like to copy to your iPhone

Camera Roll ✓

Messages ✓

Google Account ✓

Contacts ✓

Bookmarks ✓

Your android will now start moving the data to the iPhone and put the files in the right apps. Tap Continue iPhone Setup to finish the setup when the transfer is complete.

How to Turn Haptic Feedback On And Off

- Go to Settings, then tap on Sounds & Haptics.

- Scroll down and turn System Haptics off or on.

When System Haptics is off, your phone won't vibrate if you have incoming calls and alerts. If you can't hear incoming calls and alerts, open Control Center and check if Do Not Disturb is on. If it is turned on, tap to turn it off.

Lock Screen Features

Your iPhone can keep you updated on important information. On your iPhone's lock screen, you can view your emails, important messages, and much more. But with the default iOS settings, your phone might display private data on the lock screen that you don't want your friends to see. Thankfully, you have several privacy settings that help you control what info can be seen on the screen. I'm going to show you which settings to change to keep your data private off your lock screen.

- Lock Screen Notifications: This displays several notifications on the lock screen when your iPhone wakes up. To hide these notifications, head to Settings, then to Touch ID and Passcode or Face ID and Passcode, Scroll down to "Allow Access When Locked settings". As you can see below, there are several information you can disable.

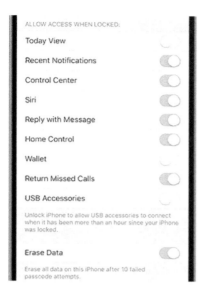

- Today View: this allows you to view widgets when you swipe to the right of your iPhone display without unlocking it. But if this feature is on, anyone who has your phone can also view this data. Depending on your widgets, friends can view your private info and notifications from your apps.

- Recent Notifications: These can be email alerts or messages that can show the entire messages, and other messages from any app that displays notifications. Turn this off to hide lock screen notifications.

- Control Center: With this, you can turn Bluetooth or Wi-Fi on and off, control music playback and brightness, turn flashlight on, and more. You can't access your personal info from the "Control Center".

- Siri: Using Siri from the lock screen is risky as friends can find out some of your information, send messages, and also make calls. E.g. if Siri is active, you can just ask, "Who owns this device?" and your contact card will be displayed if you already have one set up. If you turn Siri off, no one can use Siri while your phone is locked.

- Reply with Message and Return Missed Calls: With both these settings, you can reply to messages or make calls without unlocking your phone.

- Wallet: Please turn this option off so that friends won't have access to your Wallet with ApplePay and your credit and debit card when your phone is locked.

iPhone Quick Action

You can access shortcuts to popular actions right from the Home screen. With a long-press on an app's icon, you can access the app's quick actions. Thanks to the Haptic Touch, you should feel a slight vibration. When you do, a menu with different options to choose from will appear including actions tailored to the app. Select any of the options to launch the app into the chosen function. These include easy access to common actions such as Take Selfie from the Camera app or Send My Location from Maps. You can either tap these options or just slide your finger to launch the action.

How to Add Widgets to Home Screen

Widgets can sit alongside your favorite apps on your home screen. And what's more, widgets now come in small, medium, and large sizes.

How to add a widget to your Home screen from the Today view

- Open "Today view" by swiping right on your Home screen.

- Hold down the widget you want to move. Drag to move the widget to your Home screen.

How to add a new widget

- Hold down anywhere on your Home screen until the apps begin to jiggle.

- Tap the + (plus) sign. Tap on any of the pre-defined widgets or tap on an app's widget. Swipe either left or right on the widget sizes to choose the size you want.

- Tap and drag the widget you chose to a position on the Home screen.

- Tap "Done"

How to edit a widget

- Hold down on a widget or Smart Stack until the context menu shows up.

- Tap on "Edit Widget". If you're editing a single widget in a Smart Stack, you tap Edit "[Widget name]".

- Use the options to tune the widget the way you want. Each widget has several options.

How to add a widget to the Today view

- Open the "Today view". Hold down your screen until the apps begin to jiggle.

- Tap on the + (plus) button and tap on the app's widget you want to move.

- Swipe either left or right on the widget sizes to choose the size you want. Tap and drag the widget to the Today view.

- To exit, tap Done.

How to remove widgets from the Home screen

- Hold down the widget until the context menu appears.

- Tap on Remove Widget. Tap Remove.

CHAPTER 4: HOW TO USE APPS

How to Close Apps

- Head to the app and hold the long line at the end of your screen with a finger.

- Slide the line upwards to close the app.

How to Close multiple Apps

- Open your home screen and slide the screen upwards from the bottom with your fingers.

- You will see all the apps you opened running in the background.

- Slide each app upwards to close them.

How to Download and Install Apps

Apps installed from the App Store either appear on your Home screen or on a subsequent screen of apps. First, you need to search for cool apps to get them:

- Head to the App Store and tap on the magnifying glass at the bottom of your screen (the search button).
- Type in the app you want to search for and tap the search button.

How to download apps and games

- Tap on the app or game you searched for (it could be free or you'll need to purchase it).
- If it is free tap on Get it or tap on the price if it is paid.
- Next, activate Touch ID by Double-clicking the side button for Face ID or place your finger on the Home button.

How to manually update games and apps

- Go to the App Store and tap on your Profile icon. Head to "Update" for apps that need updates.

How to run automatic update

- Launch Settings and tap on iTunes and App Store.

- Scroll to automatic downloads and switch App Updates on.

How to disable app updates over cellular

If you are concerned about using your data to download updates, especially if automatic updates are on, you should disable it.

1. Head to Settings and tap on iTunes and App Store.

2. Under Cellular Data, turn the Automatic Downloads switch off.

How to Subscribe to Apple Arcade

- Head to the app store and look down to the bottom you will see the arcade button.

- You can do a free trial for a month. Click try free and agree to the "T&C"

- Tap on Subscribe to start a monthly subscription. Review the subscription detail and confirm with your ID.

How to Cancel your Apple Arcade Subscription

1. Go to App Store and tap on your profile icon

2. Tap on Subscriptions, then on "Apple Arcade" and then tap on Cancel Subscription.

You can't play any Arcade games after you have canceled your subscription. You can re-subscribe to play the games and regain access to your gameplay data. You might lose some of your gameplay data if you don't re-subscribe on time.

Camera App

iPhone 12 camera app has been updated to take advantage of Apple's latest features such as night mode portraits and Dolby Vision HDR recording. Below is the best way to take advantage of what the Camera app has to offer. The cameras and the camera app are full of features, much of which Apple doesn't tell you about. Although there are several features and various ways to use them. Each feature is designed to make taking pictures more convenient, efficient, and faster.

Volume buttons

This is commonly used by many, yet some may be ignorant of this handy trick. In the camera app, you can use the volume buttons as shutter buttons. Whenever you open the camera app, click on either of the volume buttons to take a picture. If you hold either of the volume buttons, a video recording will start. You can change it if you don't want it this way. Go to Settings and set the up button to capture burst photos. You can now take burst photos when you hold and release the up volume button.

More QuickTake Options

QuickTake is a modification of holding the volume button to capture videos and a faster way to take photos or videos. You can tap the "Shutter" to take a photo or hold the "Shutter" to start a video recording without switching to video mode. That's cool for really fast videos but not great for shooting long videos. If you plan on recording a lengthy video and don't want to hold the shutter the whole time, hold the "shutter" and slide it to the right to lock it in video mode. If you hold and swipe the shutter button to the left, you will start taking burst mode photos until you let up.

Adjusting the Scope

iPhone 12 and 12 mini has two cameras: the ultra-wide and wide-angle lens. The ultra-wide lens can scope out from 1X to 5X digital zoom.

To quickly switch from 1X to 5X and back again, you can just tap on the 1X icon. You can also hold down and slide your finger to the left to bring up a wheel with more granular levels of zoom. iPhone 12 Pro and Pro Max have three cameras: ultra-wide, wide, and tele lenses. Then, the camera app shows 5X, 1X, and 2X options instead of just one zoom level indicator, and selecting one lets the iPhone switch between cameras.

Portrait Mode

Thanks to the LiDAR scanner, you can take portrait shots in low light. Night mode portraits can only be taken at 1X.

Night Mode

Night mode is now available on all lenses and when the light is right, it is automatically activated, but you can also manually turn it on and off. You can also access the night mode in the tool tray.

Dolby Vision

Shooting with this feature is a big deal for videographers. You can switch this on from Settings.

How to toggle Dolby Vision recording on

- Go to Settings, then to Camera, and then go to record video.

- Switch on HDR Video.

Now, you can shoot a video in Dolby Vision HDR. If you've recorded a video in Dolby Vision HDR, you'll see an HDR indicator at the top left of the thumbnail in the Photos app.

Final notes and minor features

Apple has unveiled its Smart HDR 3 and the scene recognition mode with these latest phones. For instance, it can properly expose a portrait, or adjust the color and contrast on a photo of food, or improve saturation on a landscape shot. HDR is still going to be used, but you can also disable scene recognition within the camera settings.

Next, the magic of Apple's computational photography is Deep Fusion and it previously worked only on a wide lens. Now it works on the ultra-wide and front cameras. Any shots with these will automatically make the image better.

Apple ProRAW is a new feature that will be added to iPhone 12 Pro and Pro Max in the next few months and you can get this when you run a software update. Apple puts tremendous importance on the camera app and does its best to make sure you always take the best image possible.

How to Switch Between Apps

On previous iPhones, you had to invoke the quick app switcher to swipe back and forth between apps. With the new iPhone 12, you can do it a lot faster.

- Use your finger to touch the gesture area at the bottom of the iPhone display.

- Swipe from left to right to return to the previous app or swipe from right to left to return to the next app.

How to multitask with App switcher

You can use "App Switcher" to easily swap between apps without having to close them.

- Swipe up from the bottom until you get half-way of the screen to launch the "App Switcher".

- This will display your apps in the order they were opened, each looking like a screenshot.

- Swipe up any app to force close it. You can use two fingers to close multiple apps at a time – simply swipe up using the same motion to close them.

How to Dictate Text

If you are not a fan of typing, you can dictate your messages and have them written out as text. Just tap on the microphone icon next to the spacebar and start speaking. Click on Done once you are through with your speech. To include punctuation, just say the word. For instance, for the sentence "Hi Josh, how are you?" you would say, "Hi Josh comma how are you question mark." You can even say "new paragraph" to add a new line

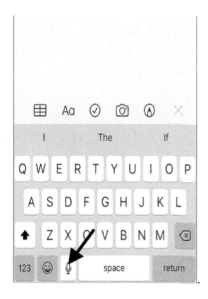

If you can't find the microphone icon on your keyboard, you will need to enable dictation.

- Head to Settings, then select General and then Keyboards. Activate 'Enable Dictation".

How to Use the New Messages features

Messages used to be a handy replacement for the limited and costly text messaging, but with the new iPhone, it has evolved into a powerful communication tool. Apple may have made more upgrades and additions to Messages with iOS 14 than it did with any other part of the new operating system. You can also organize a chat by naming it.

How to name a group conversation

- Open the Message app and open any group conversation.

- Tap on the images of people in it. Tap on the i button

- Select Change Name and Photo. Select enter a Group Name and rename the group

- Tap "Done". You can also set up a new profile image for the group chat.

How to pin a group conversation

- Select any message and swipe from left to right. Tap on the yellow pin icon to pin the chat

The pinned conversation will appear at the top of your Message screen. To un-pin the chat, hold down on that icon and choose Unpin from the menu that appears. You can also choose to hide alerts from the same menu.

There are moments in a chat where you will be needed or moments where you don't want to miss something being said. This is where you use mentions.

How to see mentions

- Head to settings, select messages, scroll to "Notify Me" and turn it on. Now when anyone mentions your name, you will receive a notification.

How to get someone's attention in Messages

- Type their name and the text will turn gray

- Tap on the gray text, press the space bar and an icon with their image will appear.

- Tap on the icon and the gray name will turn blue with a brief animation

- Now, type your message. That's it

Although, there is an easier way to go about it which common to WhatsApp users. Type the @ symbol followed by the name of the person, press the space bar and their name will turn blue with a little animation. Messages will remove the @ symbol. You can now tap any chat and respond to that comment using inline instead of going through everyone's comments.

How to use inline replies

- Go to the conversation and hold on to the comment.

- Choose "Reply" from the menu and type your message. Your reply will be shown underneath the chat you are referring to.

How to Use Keyboard Shortcuts

For example, typing out your email address that's about 25 characters long can be shortened to just a few words. That's a lot less work. You can custom your keyboard shortcuts for almost anything. To create a keyboard shortcut:

- Head to settings, then tap General and then tap "Keyboard." Tap on "Text Replacement"

- You will see Apple's shortcut example "On my way!" using "omw" as the shortcut

- Tap the plus icon to customize your shortcut and then type in a Phrase and Shortcut.

- Tap "Save".

- You can cancel by selecting "Text Replacement" to return to the list of currently saved custom replacements.

How to delete Unwanted Shortcuts

Swipe to the left on the shortcut. A short swipe will display the "Delete" button and a long swipe will automatically delete the shortcut.

How to Add or Change Keyboard

There are hundreds of foreign-language keyboards on your iPhone with which you can type.

How to change your keyboard

iPhone gives you access to more than 80 keyboards in foreign languages. Here's how to use them.

- Head to Settings, then to General, and then tap Keyboard.

- Tap on Keyboards and then select "Add New Keyboard" from the keyboard page.

- Find and select your desired keyboard, then tap "Done."

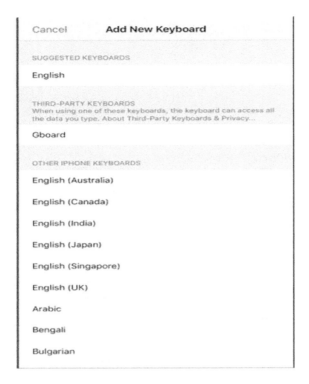

- Your new keyboard will appear on your keyboard list, along with your default and Emoji keyboard.

How to change to a third-party keyboard

There are lots of keyboards to download in the App Store which gives you several options to interact with your device. Here's how to use them.

- Head to the app store and download any keyboard of your choice.

- Launch the keyboard app and follow any instructions that pops up. In some cases, you need to go to settings, find the keyboard, and enable features.

- Head to Settings, then to General, and then tap on Keyboard. Select "Add New Keyboard" from the keyboard page

- Search for your new keyboard In the Third-Party Keyboards section and tap it.

Cancel   **Add New Keyboard**

SUGGESTED KEYBOARDS

English

THIRD-PARTY KEYBOARDS
When using of these keyboards, the keyboard can access all the data y e. About Third-Party Keyboards & Privacy...

Gboard

OTHER IPHONE KEYBOARDS

English (Australia)

English (Canada)

English (India)

English (Japan)

English (Singapore)

English (UK)

Arabic

Bengali

Bulgarian

- Tap the new keyboard from the list and if needed, allow access.

How to use a new keyboard after you've changed to it

Launch an app like "WhatsApp" that you can type. Tap or tap and hold the globe shaped button at the bottom to use it. Works both ways

How to change your default keyboard

- Go to Settings, then to General, and then tap on Keyboard.

- Tap on Keyboards and then from the keyboard page, tap "Edit."

- Rearrange the keyboard. You can arrange them by dragging three horizontal lines on the right side of your screen. Drag the preferred keyboard to the top of the list.

- Tap "Done."

How to Use iPhone Search

Search helps you to locate anything on your device and the web easily.

- Swipe down from the middle of the Home screen and tap the Search field

- Type what you are searching for. You'll notice live search updates as you type.

- Tap on show more to see more search results or you can search directly in an app by tapping Search in app.

- Tap on a search result to open it.

How to change search settings

You limit the apps and results that appear when you are searching. Here's how:

- Go to Settings and tap Siri and Search.

- Select an app and then select Suggest App

- Select show app in search, then select show content in search or suggest shortcuts for app.

To turn off Siri Suggestions for all apps:

- Head to Settings then tap on Siri and Search.

- Turn off any of the settings.

How to Use Airdrop to Send Items to Other Device

With AirDrop, you can quickly and efficiently transfer files across your friend's apple device. If you can't find your friend as a nearby AirDrop user, tell them to open Control Center and allow AirDrop to receive files. Here is how to go about it

- Open "Control Center". Turn Bluetooth and Wi-Fi on. Next, enable AirDrop and select either "Contacts Only" or "Everyone". Everyone is much easier to use.

- To AirDrop photos, head to the Photos app and mark the photos, tap the "Share button", then choose "AirDrop" and select the target device. Next, tap "Accept" to receive the file.

- To AirDrop contacts, head to the Contacts app, mark the contact, tap "Share Contact", and then select the target device. Tap "Accept" on the target device to receive the contact. You can only send one contact at a time which can be stressful sometimes.

How to Draw In Apps with Markup

Markup is a handy in-built image-annotation feature that allows you to edit images, add text, add a signature to a PDF, and create drawings.

How to use markup's menu tools

Here's how to get started with Markup's basic tools.

- Take a screenshot and quickly tap on the screenshot's thumbnail preview as it will disappear in about 5 seconds.

- You'll see the Markup's interface with the tools at the bottom.

- Tap the plus or cross sign to display the Signature, Text, Magnifier, and Opacity tools.

- Tap the Highlighter or Pen and then draw what you want on the screenshot.

- Tap the same tool again to change its opacity. Tap on the Eraser to erase, and then rub your finger along the areas.

- To move an object or shape you've drawn, tap the Lasso tool, and then use your finger to make a circle around the drawing.

You'll see a dotted line circling the drawing. Drag it to another part of the screen.

- To change the color of your Highlighter or Pen, tap the color wheel at the bottom.

How to use markup's additional tools

- If you would like to do more with Markup, tap the plus or cross sign.

- To type something on your screenshot, Tap "Text". Tap the text symbol (a capital A) to change the size, font, and style of the text. Tap inside the text box to type. Tap and drag the text box where you want it on the screen. Tap the color wheel to change the color of the text.

- Tap on Magnifier to adjust the size of your image or just a portion of the image.

- To zoom in, use the green circle and use the blue circle to enlarge the area of the magnified image.

- Tap Opacity, and move the slider to adjust the transparency level of your image.

- Markup also allows you to add a signature as well. Tap the plus (+) sign and then tap on Signature. Draw a signature and then tap Done.

- You can also move the signature, change its color and size. The signature will be saved and available on other photos or documents.

How to use markup's shape tools

- Tap the plus or cross sign and then tap the square, circle, speech bubble, or arrow shape to add an adjustable arrow to the image.

- When you're done editing, tap Done and then select Save to Photos, Save to Files, or Delete.

How to use markup when emailing a photo

- Open the Mail app and compose a new email or open an existing email. Tap the body of the email to display a menu bar. Tap the arrow until it displays Insert Photo or Video.

- Select it and it will take you to your Photo Library.

- Select a photo and tap "Choose" to add it to the email.

- Tap the image in the email to display the menu bar. Select Markup.

- Use the Markup tools to edit the photo and tap Done. Type the email's message and then Send.

How to use markup with notes

- Open a Note and tap the Markup icon

- Use the Markup tools to annotate the note or add a drawing. Tap Done.

How to Perform Quick Actions with Back Tap

There are two quick-action shortcuts that can be triggered when you double or triple-tap on the back of your phone.

- Go to Settings, then to Accessibility, and then to Select Touch.

- Scroll down to the Back Tap option

- Hit 'Double Tap' and select a desired quick action.

- Go back and do the same thing for Triple Tap'.

How to Use and Customize Control Center

Apple added some new features to the Control Center and also improved how you can customize it.

How to choose Home devices for Control Center

- Open the Home app and tap the Home icon to choose a room.

- Hold down one of the accessories from the list and tap the gear icon.

- Turn on "Include in Favorites". Tap the X button to close

Although, there is a quicker way:

- Launch Control Center and tap the Home Favorites button

- Tap on the Home icon.

This will take you directly to the Home app and save you the stress of coming out of Control Center to find apps separately. You can have as many Favorites as you want but, you will find them in the Home Favorites screen not in Control Center.

How to customize Control Center

- Head to Settings, then to "Control Center" and then choose the Included Controls top list or customize controls.

- Tap the red minus (-) sign if you want to remove a control or use the grab handles to rearrange the controls.

- Choose the More Controls second list and tap the green plus sign (+) next to any control you want.

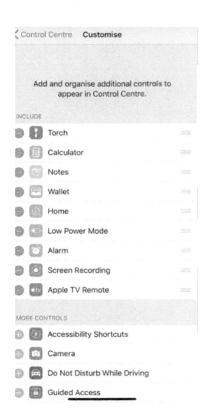

While the Control Center has vertically arranged icons, you can change its arrangement by editing a list of controls. When you drag a control to the top of the list, it will go to the top of the "Control Center".

Extra settings in Control Center

A long-press on any of the controls reveals many more options. For example, you get 2 more controls for tapping the main set with Wi-Fi, Airplane mode, and so on. Or a long press on Do Not Disturb gives you the option to temporarily turn the feature on.

How to Choose Settings for Travel

On every iOS update, Apple always adds new features to its built-in apps, and iOS 14 is no exception. Many apps, including Apple Maps, have new important features that include cycling routes, EV routes, guides, and more.

How to bring up your current location

- Go to Maps and choose the location icon at the top right.

How to mark your current location

- Tap your current location and Select "Mark My Location".

How to share my current location

- Go to Maps and tap your current location. Select "Share My Location".

- Select how to share your location from the options in the share sheet. You can share your location through Reminders, social networks, etc.

How to change your map view

Your options include the default, Transit, and Satellite view:

- Go to Maps and search for a location.

- Tap the "information" icon and choose your preferred view.

How to browse or search for a location

Using Search

- Go to Maps and find an address using the Search box.

- Tap the location to view it on a map and select directions to path your trip (if applicable).

Find nearby locations

- Go to Maps and select the location icon at the top right so that the map is centered on your current location.

- Select the Search box. Choose from any of the categories under "Find Nearby". For instance, tap Hotel to find hotels near your current location to lodge.

- Choose any location you find under the category you selected earlier.

- Choose "Directions" to get more info of your location.

Use Siri suggestions and previous location

You will also see a listing of Siri's suggestions and previous locations on the main Maps screen. Simply tap on the listed site to get more info.

How to select a route in Maps

- Go to Maps and find an address via the Search box. Select "Directions" to path your trip. Select the path you want on the map.

How to add or remove a stop on your route

Maps offer an easy search button to the nearest gas stations, hotels, and restaurants while you're on the road.

- In the Map's directions mode, swipe up on the bottom toolbar to display more options.

- Tap on a "Location". You can scroll through the pop-over to view locations and their route time. Tap the "Go" button to put a stop on your route and the stop will be added.

- Tap on "Resume Route To banner" to remove the stop.

How to view your full route on the map or in text form

You can use the Overview button to get a birds' eye view of your route.

- In the Map's directions mode, swipe up on the bottom toolbar to display more options.

- Tap the "Overview button" to zoom out the map area. This will show your full trip.

- To return to the turn-by-turn map screen, swipe up on the bottom toolbar and press Resume.

If you want to see your full route as turn-by-turn text directions instead:

- In the Map's directions mode, swipe up on the bottom toolbar to display more options.

- Tap "Details" to display the full list of directions. Tap "Done" to return to the turn-by-turn map screen.

How to change the guidance volume for your directions

- In the Map's directions mode, swipe up on the bottom toolbar to display more options.

- Tap "Audio" and choose which voice preference you prefer under the "Navigation Voice preferences". After choosing an audible direction option, you can also pause spoken audio when the voice the app's voice interjects.

How to take portrait photos

- Head to the Camera app and select Portrait mode.

- Follow the commands on your screen to frame the subject in the yellow portrait box.

- Drag the Portrait Lighting control icon ⬡ to choose a lighting effect:

- Tap the "Shutter" to capture.

If you don't like an image you captured in Portrait mode, you can edit it by going to the Photos app, open the photo, tap on Edit and then tap on Portrait to turn the effect on or off.

How to adjust depth control in portrait mode

- Go to "Camera", select Portrait mode, and then frame your subject.

- Tap on "Depth Adjustment" *f*. The Depth Control slider will appear below the frame.

- Drag the slider either to the left or right to adjust the effect. Tap on the "Shutter" to capture.

In Photos, you can further adjust the background blur effect of a Portrait image using the Depth Control slider.

How to adjust portrait lighting effects in portrait mode

- Go to the camera app, select Portrait mode, and then drag the Portrait Lighting control icon ⬡ to choose a lighting effect.

- Tap on the Portrait Control button ⬡. Drag the slider either to the left or right to adjust the effect. Tap the "Shutter" to capture

In Photos, you can further adjust the lighting effect of a Portrait image using the Portrait Lighting slider.

How to Take an HDR Photo

You need to check your HDR settings in settings before going to the Camera app.

- Go to Settings, then to Camera, and then ensure you switch off Smart HDR. You won't see the HDR option in the Camera app if Smart HDR is on.

- Switch on Keep Normal Photo. This informs your iPhone to save a non-HDR version of the photo.

- Close Settings and open the "Camera". Ensure the HDR icon is on (the icon appears without a line through it when it's on).

- After you switch HDR on, your phone will automatically capture HDR photos. Capturing an HDR picture takes a little longer than a normal one. This is because the camera has to capture three images at several exposures and merge them into a single photo.

- Because of the extra time required, it is advisable to mount your phone on a tripod as any movement would result in a blurred photo caused by camera shake.

How to Scan a QR Code

These days, QR codes appear more and more frequently. The square pixel graphics are basically smartphone barcodes, programmed to display a specific response when scanned. They are also used to direct viewers to a website and can also be used to connect to a Wi-Fi network easily. All you need to do is open Camera, point your camera at the QR code, and then tap on the notification that pops up on the screen. Your device will automatically launch whatever it is the QR code is about

CHAPTER FIVE: INTERNET AND CALLS

How to Share Internet

Fortunately, you can share Wi-Fi and surf the internet with your iPhone hotspot:

- First, check if your mobile connection is activated. Now, open settings and tap on Personal Hotspot.

- Toggle on the option "Allow Others to Join". Your phone will automatically generate a password for the Wi-Fi connection. Click on 'password and modify' if you want to change the password. Now, the option to share your internet connection is activated, you must configure this Wi-Fi connection on the other device.

To connect via Wi-Fi:

Select the device name in the Wi-Fi settings of your other device from which you want to connect to the internet. Enter your hotspot password when required.

To connect via Bluetooth:

- Link your iPhone to the computer. On your phone, press the link or enter the code that appears on the computer.

- Now connect your phone to the computer.

To connect via USB:

- Plug in your phone to the computer. Choose your device from the list of network services.

- Your device has the following network connectivity to be able to share the internet: GSM / CDMA / HSPA / EVDO / LTE / 5G.

- 2G connectivity: GSM 850 / 900 / 1800 / 1900 - SIM 1 & SIM 2 (dual-SIM) - for China. 3G connectivity: HSDPA 850 / 900 / 1700(AWS) / 1900 / 2100. 4G connectivity: LTE.

How to Receive Calls

An incoming call can be answered, silenced, or declined. If a call is declined, it goes to voicemail. You can also use a text to respond.

How to receive a call

- Tap on the call icon or drag the slider if the device is locked.

- You can have your iPhone announce all incoming calls or only calls you receive while using headphones or Bluetooth in your car. Open Settings, go to Phone and then to "Announce Calls".

Silence a call

Press either the side button, Sleep/Wake button or the volume button.

How to decline a call and send it to voicemail

You can either:

- Press the side or Sleep/Wake button twice quickly.

- Tap on the decline call button . Swipe up on the call banner.

How to create a default reply,

- Open Settings, go to Phone and then to "Respond with Text".

- Tap any default message and replace it with your text.

How to Avoid Unwanted Calls

First, you need to download a spam blocking and call identifying app with good reviews, e.g., Nomorobo, TrueCaller, and Hiya.

- Once you have downloaded the app, go to Settings and then scroll down to "Call Blocking and Identification".

- You should see the app you downloaded as an option in this section. Switch the toggle on so the app can start blocking your spam calls.

- If the spam numbers are not on the app's list, it may not block all calls.

How to Setup Face Time

Apple's FaceTime app allows you to make video or audio calls to any of your friends and family, as long as they have an iPhone. Using your phone's front camera and FaceTime, you can talk to friends face to face. Or, you can switch to the rear camera so that you can both see what's in front of you. When setting up FaceTime, just make sure you have a cellular connection or a Wi-Fi connection. You can also choose which number you want your friends to use to contact you over FaceTime.

- Head to Settings, then scroll down to FaceTime. Toggle on the FaceTime switch.

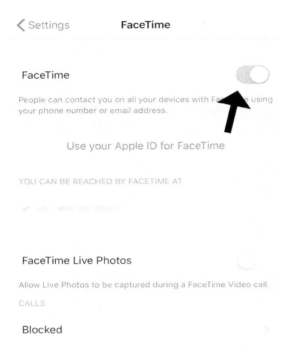

- Sign into FaceTime with your Apple ID or tap on use other Apple ID and enter the details.

- Select the phone number and/or email that you want your friends to contact you with via FaceTime.

- Select a number or email for your Caller ID. Turn "FaceTime Live Photos" on to allow your friends to take live photos during FaceTime calls.

Note: You can block friends from contacting you over FaceTime, phone calls, messages, and email by tapping on "Blocked Contacts" and adding the contacts you want to block.

How to Make a Group Face Time Call

You can initiate a Group FaceTime call via the FaceTime app or the Messages app.

FaceTime App

- Head to the FaceTime app and tap on the "+" plus button.

- Type a name in the "To:" field and tap it. Continue typing the names of all the participants you want to chat with.

- Tap the audio or video option when you are ready to place the call and participants will receive a notification that you want to FaceTime with them.

Messages App

- Create a new iMessage chat thread or open a former multi-person conversation.

- Tap the participant's name to bring up a menu bar.

- Choose the "FaceTime" option to switch to a video or audio call.

You can add another participant to an ongoing FaceTime call:

- In an ongoing call, tap the three dots icon.

- Tap "Add Person." and select a name from the list.

How to Take Live Photo

- Head to Camera and ensure your camera is set to photo mode.

- Next, tap the live photo icon to enable live photo and then tap the "Shutter" to shoot a live photo.

Hands Off Task Between IPhone And Mac

You can switch to another device and continue from where you left off. You can use Handoff with several Apple apps— Mail, Safari, Maps, Messages, Calendar, etc., and even some third-party apps. You must sign in with the same Apple ID on all your devices before you can use Handoff. You must turn on Bluetooth and be within Bluetooth range.

How to switch devices

- From Mac to iPhone: Head to App Switcher on your iPhone and tap on the Handoff icon at the bottom of your screen to continue working in the app.

- From iPhone to Mac: Tap the Handoff icon that appears in the Dock on your Mac to continue working in the app.

How to Disable Handoff on your devices

- iPhone: Head to Settings, tap on General, and then tap on AirPlay and Handoff.

- Mac: Select Apple Menu, System Preferences, and then General. Turn off "Allow Handoff between this Mac and your iCloud devices."

How to Sync iPhone with Your Computer

If you are using a Windows PC, use iTunes to sync contents to your devices. Before you use iTunes to sync your content, consider using Apple Music, iCloud, or similar services to keep contents from your Mac or PC in the cloud. This way, you can have access to your files on your devices when you are not close to your computer. If you use iCloud or other services to update your content across all of your devices, certain syncing features via iTunes might be turned off. With iTunes, you can sync your Albums, songs, playlists, films, TV shows, podcasts audiobooks photos, videos, contacts, and calendar.

How to Sync or remove content using iTunes

- Open iTunes and connect your device to the computer via a USB cable.

- Click on the device icon and then from the list under Settings, select what you want to sync or remove. To turn sync on for a certain type of content, select the checkbox next to Sync.

- Click on the checkbox next to the items you want to sync.

- Click on Apply. Click the Sync button if syncing doesn't start automatically.

How to Sync via Wi-Fi

After you have set up syncing with iTunes, you can set up iTunes to sync via Wi-Fi instead of USB.

- Connect your phone to the computer via a USB cable, open iTunes, and select the device.

- Click on "Summary" on the left side of the iTunes window.

- Click on "Sync with this device over Wi-Fi". Click Apply.

Your device will appear in iTunes if it has the same Wi-Fi network as your computer. The device will automatically sync whenever it is plugged into power and iTunes is open on your computer.

Transfer Files between iPhone And Your Computer with ITunes

iTunes File Sharing is designed to share files between your computer and your iPhone. If you are sure your files were made by a compatible app, then you can use this feature.

- Connect your phone to the computer via a USB and launch iTunes.

- Click on the "Device" tab in the iTunes window and select "File Sharing".

- Select the app from which you want to transfer files to the PC.

- Select the files you want to transfer and click "Save to".

- Choose a location to save the files and click "Save to" to start transferring the files.

CHAPTER SIX UNDERSTANDING VARIOUS APPS

Calendar Events

How to create an event

- Head to the Calendar app and tap on the plus sign.

- This will take you to the event creation screen. Give your entry a title, date, time, and also an address under location if you like.

- If you want it to be an all-day event, choose that. Turn off this option if your event already has time. Next, you'll see dates and times which you can edit.

- Go to "Repeat" if you want to customize and repeat events.

- Tap on Invitees to share a calendar event with a friend.

- Next, choose an alert and a second alert if want to receive event notifications.

- If you set up several calendars, tap "Calendar" to add an event to a specific one.

- Type in the URLs or notes. Tap "Done" to save.

How to edit an event

- Go to the Calendar app and tap on the entry you want to edit.

- Tap on Edit and edit anything you need to.

- Tap "Done" to save.

How to Set an Alarm

Among the more modest tweaks is a redesigned Clock app. The clock app on this device is simpler but also a bit counterintuitive in others.

How to use alarms

- Head to the Clock app and tap on the "Alarm tab".

- Tap the plus +" icon or hit Edit and tap on an existing alarm to modify it

- Use the number keypad to enter your alarm time or you can swipe up or down on the orange time to use it as a wheel picker.

- Tap Save

- You can also use Siri to set alarms or the Sleep Schedule feature

If you start by tapping the orange alarm time at the top, only the hour or minutes to be edited will be selected. However, you can use the number pad to quickly enter the time for your alarm.

How to Use the Timer or Stopwatch

How to set the timer

- Head to the Clock app and tap on Timer. Set the time and sound to play when the timer ends.

- Tap Start.

If you want to fall asleep while using media, you can set the timer to stop the playback. Tap "When Timer Ends" and then tap "Stop Playing". The time will continue even if the device goes to sleep or if you open another app.

How to use a stopwatch

- Tap the Stopwatch and swipe the stopwatch to switch between the digital and analog. Tap on Start.

- Tap on Lap to record a lap or split. Tap "Stop" to record the final time and tap "Reset" to clear the stopwatch.

How to Play Music

- Click on the Music icon. This will open up the Library view. When you open the Music App the first time, you may see a screen telling you to sign up for Apple Music. You can ignore and dismiss this for now.

- Enter the Library interface.

- Choose from any of these options: Playlists, Artists, Albums, Songs, Genres, Compilations, and Downloaded Music.

- You will also see Recently Added. Tap on Songs, here you will see all the tracks.

How to Subscribe to Apple Music

- Go to iTunes or the Apple Music app. Or go to music.apple.com to subscribe.

- Go to Listen Now or For You and tap the trial offer.

- Choose a subscription (individual, family, or student). You can share your family subscription with six people.

- Sign in with your Apple ID or create a new one if you don't have one.

- Confirm your billing details and add a payment method. Tap or click Join.

How to Add Siri

How to perform a Siri query in iOS 14

- If you enabled verbal triggers, start by stating "Hey Siri" followed by your question.

- You can also hold down the Side button, the Home Button, or in some iPad Pro models, the Top button, followed by your query.

- Siri will automatically respond or perform the task once the query is made.

You can extend Siri's time if the timing out is too early. Simply hold the Side, Top, or Home button during the query. Release the button when you are done.

How to adjust Siri

- Go to Settings and then to Siri and Search.

- Make the necessary changes to Siri and then exit Settings.

Tell Siri about Yourself

- Head to Settings and tap on Siri and Search. Tap on My Information and choose your contact entry.

You can then say, "Remind me to meet Danny for lunch," and Siri will set the alert to go off at the registered location.

Advanced contact details

Siri will know more about you if you add extra details about a contact. Start Siri and then tell it a contact's name followed by their relationship to you. E.g. "Kathrin Evans is my best friend." Siri will then ask you to confirm your relationship with Kathrin. You can say, "Call Dad" or "email girlfriend" and it will know who to contact.

How to Use Siri in Your Car

If you've never used CarPlay, you need to pair the two devices first. So, connect your phone to the car. If wireless CarPlay is available, hold down the voice button on your steering wheel to launch the configuration. Then on your device:

- Head to Settings and tap your car's name

- Then go to General and then to CarPlay. That's it!

CHAPTER SEVEN: SECURITY

How to Use Security Features

To better secure your iPhone, Apple's iOS 14 offers several new protection and privacy features. One of iOS 14's very useful tool is the Security Recommendations menu, which helps to identify weak or compromised passwords so that you can update them and prevent hacking of your accounts. You can create more complex passwords with the latest iOS 14 iCloud Keychain tool, alerting you that you need to change your credentials if it detects a breach. So, how does it work?

- Go to Settings, then to Passwords, and then to Security Recommendations.

- Make sure "Detect Compromised Passwords" is on. If you turn this on, your phone will securely monitor your passwords.

- If you have any issues with your passwords, Apple will sort these into "High Priority" and "Other Recommendations."

Suggestions may involve changing re-used passwords, this is important since the attacker may try to use this to hack your other services through "credential stuffing" once any of your accounts is compromised.

How to Force Restart

How to turn the device off then on again

- Simultaneously hold down the volume up button and side buttons for few seconds.

- Slide the on-screen power symbol ⏻ to the right.

- Hold the side button until the Apple logo appears to turn it back on.

This method carries out a graceful shutdown followed by the usual turn-on process. I recommend trying to use this method to solve the issue first.

How to force restart

- Quickly press and release the volume up button, followed by the volume down button.

- Hold down the side button and release it when the Apple logo appears.

Although this method will try to restart your device, the issue might not actually be resolved. If the iPhone does not turn back on, Apple's support pages give more tips, including how to recover the device in more serious cases.

Note: when restarting your device, make sure to pay attention and follow all instructions properly. Specifically the case if you confuse the two instructions and end up holding down the up volume and side buttons for a long time. In doing so, the Emergency SOS feature will begin a five-second countdown, where it will count down from five and vibrate with each number as the Emergency SOS slider fills up. If the counter gets to 0 and you are still holding both buttons down, your phone will consider the bar full and dial the emergency services, which may inform the police or an ambulance to your location. Just to pay attention and if the vibration and countdown begins, release the buttons.

How to Update IOS

- Go to Settings, then to General and tap on Software Update.

- Tap "Download and Install".

- Tap on Install to update. Or you can select Later and tap on Install Tonight or Remind Me Later. If you select Install Tonight, plug your device into power before you go to bed. Your device will automatically update overnight. Enter your passcode if you are asked to.

To turn automatic updates on:

- Head to Settings, then to General, and then tap on Software Update

- Customize "Automatic Updates", then turn on "Install iOS Updates".

How to backup iPhone

You need a Wi-FI connection for this.

Back up apps

- Go to Settings and tap your Apple ID. If prompted, sign in with your Apple ID.

- Tap on iCloud and tap the slider next to the desired apps. Tap on the iCloud Backup app at the bottom of the list.

- Turn on iCloud Backup and tap on Back Up. Wait for the backup to complete.

Back up contacts

- Go to Settings and tap on your Apple ID. Sign in if prompted.

- Tap on iCloud and then switch on the Contacts slider. Select Merge contacts with iCloud if you are asked to.

- Tap on the iCloud Backup app at the bottom. Turn on iCloud Backup and tap on Back Up

- Wait for the backup to complete.

Back up media and pictures

From phone

- Go to Settings and tap on your Apple ID. Sign in if prompted.

- Tap on iCloud and then tap Photos. Turn the iCloud Photo Library slider on.

- Tap on iCloud to return to the previous screen. Next, tap the iCloud Backup app.

- Turn on iCloud Backup and tap on Back Up

- Wait for the backup to complete.

How to restore iPhone 12 To Default

A master reset restores your phone's default settings and may delete files on your internal storage

- Back up all your data on the internal memory.

- If you enabled Apple FMiP Activation Lock, you need to access the internet to complete these steps.

- Head to settings, then to general, and then select Reset.

- Select from any of the options:

1. Reset All Settings: Use this option before you attempt a master reset.

2. Erase All Content and Settings: Use this option for master reset. Make sure you select Erase all and keep plans.

3. Reset Network Settings: This will erase any saved Wi-Fi profiles.

4. Reset Keyboard Dictionary

5. Reset Home Screen Layout

6. Reset Location and Privacy

- Enter your password if you are asked to.

- Confirm your selection.

How to Restore All Contents from Backup

Option one: Erase all current data

You can restore all your data if you backed them up via iTunes. if you do a restore with iTunes, all your current data will be erased. Use the following steps:

- On your computer, open iTunes. Connect your phone to the computer and enter your passcode if you are asked to or select "Trust this Computer".

- Select the device in iTunes or the Finder window to continue.

- Click on "Select Backup" and then depending on the date, select the most relevant backup.

- Click on "Restore".

Option 2: Do not need to erase data (Recommend)

If you don't want to remove all your current data, use PanFone Data Transfer to restore it.

- Download and install PanFone on your computer. Launch the app.

- Connect your device to the computer via a USB cable.

- Click on the iTunes Backup File. Select "Restore" and click on "iTunes backup". If you have already synced your device with iTunes on the computer, then PanFone Data Transfer can detect the iTunes backup files. Click on "Next" to load iTunes backup from your computer.

- Next, all saved iTunes backups will be enlisted. Select one backup according to its date or size. Then click Start.

- Click on the Desired Contents from iTunes Backup. All data from the backup file will be available to restore. Just mark the ones you need then click "Next" to load the files. This might take a while depending on the size

- Retrieve the Files from iTunes Backup to your device. Once the data is loaded, select the files you want to retrieve then click "Recover to Computer" or "Recover to iOS 14 device" as needed. After the process is complete, your device will automatically reboot. Do not disconnect the device until the process is successful.

Printed in Great Britain
by Amazon

41291916R00081